Hearts

Jenny Lynne

Hearts
Jenny Lynne

Brazzle Publishing, Inc.

Photography: Jenny Lynne
Book Shepherd: Judith Briles, https://thebookshepherd.com
Cover, Interior design and eBook conversion: Rebecca Finkel, F + P Graphic Design
Printed by: King Printing Company, Inc.

Library of Congress Catalog Number: 2018949775

ISBN print: 978-1-7324015-0-1
ISBN ebook: 978-1-7324015-1-8

I dedicate this to my mom and dad.

Thank you for always
believing in my dreams
and encouraging
me to reach for
the stars!

I am who I am because of you and your perfect love.
You are my soul. I love you for a lifetime and beyond!

It's easy to go for a walk and get lost in thought
or stuck in a looping pattern of emotions.

I constantly remind myself to be present
and actually see what I'm seeing.

When I do,
I'm rewarded with one of nature's heart-shaped beauties
as a clear sign that love is everywhere!

. . . so off on a hike I go . . . to find my **heart** and soul.

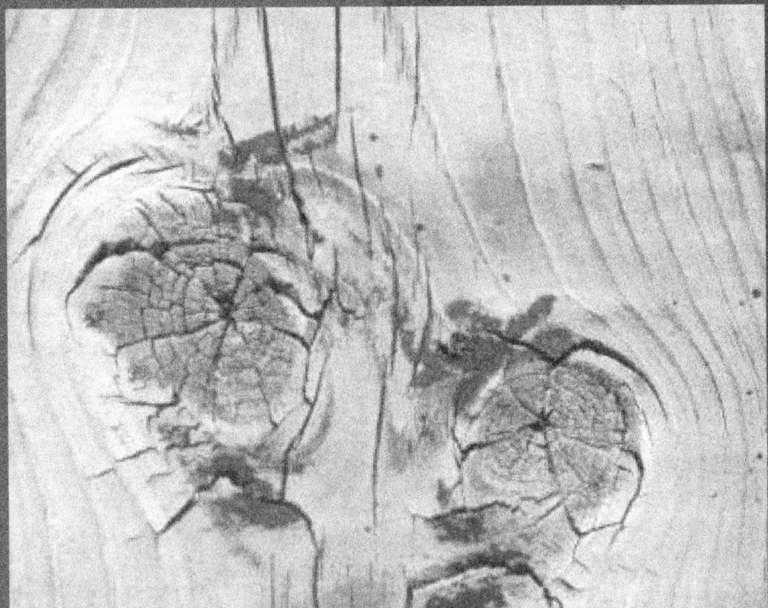

With no imagination,
would you/could you see this heart?

If each and every heart was perfect,
how would you/could you be unique?

If each and every heart was perfect,
would there/could there be intrigue?

But wait, the fact is that your heart is perfect,
so let its perfect self shine through.

After all, in a brief moment's reflection, there's no **heart** as unique as you!

A heart shaped rock, often commonly found,
is always welcomed and should be
treated like treasure when stumbled upon.

Do you pick it up and take it for yourself
or leave it in its place for others
to take pleasure in nature's largess?

There's no right or wrong answer.
The universal sign of love has its own personal meaning.
What does it mean to you?

When nature shows you a **heart**, cherish it.

My breath is constantly taken away
by nature's accidental beauty.

After an afternoon rain, there is
a heart shaped stain leaving it's heart print,
holding last remnants of moisture in the air
before it disappears as though 'twas never there.

Only the few who chose this path
during these fleeting moments,
shared space with this heart.
And even fewer were aware of its existence,
though it was right there in front of them.

Take a look around: your **heart** may find what it's looking for.

This delicate beauty blossomed into more than just a stem with perfect petals.

Two hearts grew into one.

Blooming **hearts** are bound to bear beauty.

Is this an innocent reptile
whose blood simply runs cold
or a blatantly cold-hearted snake?

Sometimes it's hard to tell the difference
when you can't see past the heart.

The **heart** can't see what really might be.

Hiking in the snow is my favorite invigorating outdoor activity.

My body is put through so many extreme elements,
from trying to keep warm
to trying not to slip and fall.

Another reason for this favored form of fitness—
I'm forced to go slow,
and at times, be precise with my steps.

Because of this, I take my time, focus on my breath and look around.
I'm acutely aware of my surroundings—
this is when I find the most hearts.

Take a deep breath, be present and your **heart** will become one with nature.

A heart can be so fragile.

There are days when it feels tender, stomped on, torn
and then just left on the side of the street ... to blow away.

There have been better days and there have been worse days
but at that very moment of being immersed with that feeling,
it seems like it's impossible to take away the dullness and bring back the shine.

The **heart**—it is resilient and wants to shimmer.

They say a pet and its owner
somehow resemble one another,
although both are completely different species.

The bond is so strong
that they take on similar personality traits. But isn't this also true
with people ... family, friends, foes, neighbors, co-workers?

Shouldn't that make us all want to be our best self
so those around us become a reflection?

Have a **heart** that others will want to mirror.

EAT YOUR

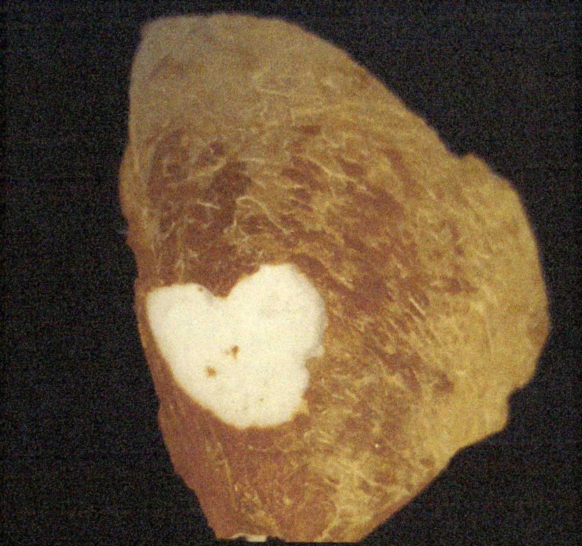

HEART OUT

Mirror mirror on the wall, who's the truest of them all?

One has left an imprint after rain
while the other lays atop rocky terrain.

One will vanish after tomorrow's stormy night
while the other will remain and can weather the fight.

Which **heart** describes you?

Nature has a sense of humor. Take the cactus for instance,
its beauty is untouchable.
You can get only so close. You can look but can't touch.

If its protection boundary is crossed, it will give you a lasting gift of piercing pain.

If you come across a **heart** that will hurt, run.

This little paper heart was on my car's floor mat
watching me speed all around town.

Somehow it didn't get trampled on by my heel.
Call it resilience or call it luck,
but it was perfectly intact when found.

Looks are deceiving.

What looks like something to be thrown away
may end up being a **heart** you want to keep.

After a night of turbulent wind, the weak, unsecured or loosely attached will be wisped, tossed, spun, whirled and thrown around, left disconnected, displaced and removed from home.

A heart needs a strong connection, something to latch onto so a gust of air won't set it in motion.

All in all, it's just another **heart** on the wall.

www.drobrand.com
COMPANY OF AMERICA
YOUNGSTOWN, OHIO.

Curly, swirly and twirly are the hairs on my head.

I opened my eyes after blow-drying and said ...
"Yup, it's going to be a good one!"

That day I wore my **heart** on my head.

Honor your heart.

Empower your heart.

Always trust your heart.

Rediscover your heart.

Teach with your heart.

Share your heart.

Hearts come in all shapes and sizes.
They are as unique as snowflakes.

Each has its own beat, its own beauty
and its own way of showing love.
They are as strong as they are fragile.
Some are yearning; some are fulfilled. Some are overflowing with love,
while others are searching for the meaning of love.
Some have a heavy heart and some are light hearted.
Some are vulnerable and some are guarded.

The more love you give; the more love you'll get.
What do we all have in common? It's to love and be loved.
Without a doubt, what the world needs is more love. So be bold!

Give your **heart** and spread the love more than you ever thought you could.

One heart,

two hearts in a tree,

just saw three hearts …

it’s meant to be!

This was one of my prouder moments of finding a heart.
It's zoomed in for you to see,
but in actuality, it was spotted from a far distance.

My eyes saw it before my mind recognized it.

I was walking fast and turned back around,
seconds after processing what it was.

I now know I'm truly in tune with finding hearts in nature.
If it's in my path, I'll see it.

Tree, leaves, soil or stone ...
a **heart** can appear in broken rock or can be grown.

Have more compassion, love and tolerance for others.
I don't make too many promises
but I do promise this will be a change for the better.

Change from your heart.
Pass it on and it will be a ripple effect.

My **heart** bleeds for you.

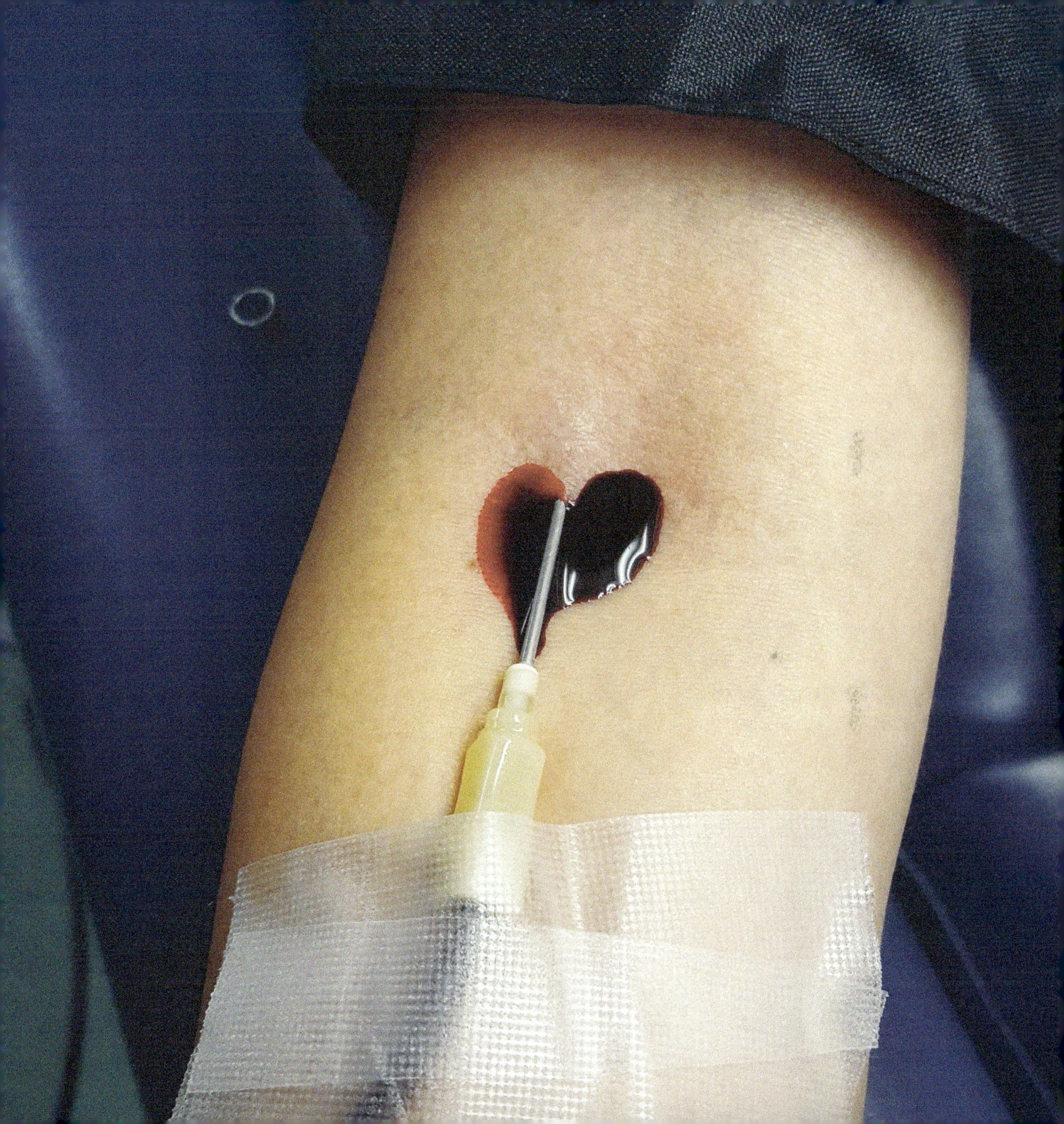

How much more can one heart take?

It may go from rock solid

to a sudden heart break.

Life is precious so live with all your **heart**.

There's a fungus among us disguised as a heart.

Don't fall for a poisonous **heart**.

This is a two-for-one special.
Look close ... closer ... do you see the heart within a heart?

Look up, look down, look all around
and you will find what you're looking for.

What's in your **heart**?

I was just chopping up some veggies
while making dinner and staring up at me
was a perfect little heart just waiting to be seen.

No meal will ever be made without a quick gaze
at the heart that will forever be there,
patiently waiting to bring a moment of joy.

Some **hearts** will last forever.

Now that I've trained my eyes,
hearts are everywhere I go.
I always smile when I find one where it's unexpected.

These are a couple of examples of accidental hearts I made.

Purposefully create a place for your **heart** to grow.

Here we go with the obvious and it might sound cliché.
I've got your heart in the palm of my hand.

Do I hold it close or keep it at bay?

Matters of the **heart.**

Here's a puddle of love overflowing from rain.

I had a playful and childish impulse to stomp on it to make a splash.

Rain, rain, go away … unless you leave a heart,
well then, we can play.

A happy heart is a playful **heart**.

Hopping around with some holiday cheer, lo and behold,
a happy heart happened to appear.

Anytime is a good time for an unexpected **heart**.

Two **hearts** appeared
on a hike through Enchanted Forest in Colorado.

Both, so temporary, and within hours will be gone.
I found it rather peculiar to see both in one day and on the same trail.

Is it a message or a sign?

I choose to believe that finding **hearts**
is a sign of an abundance of love.

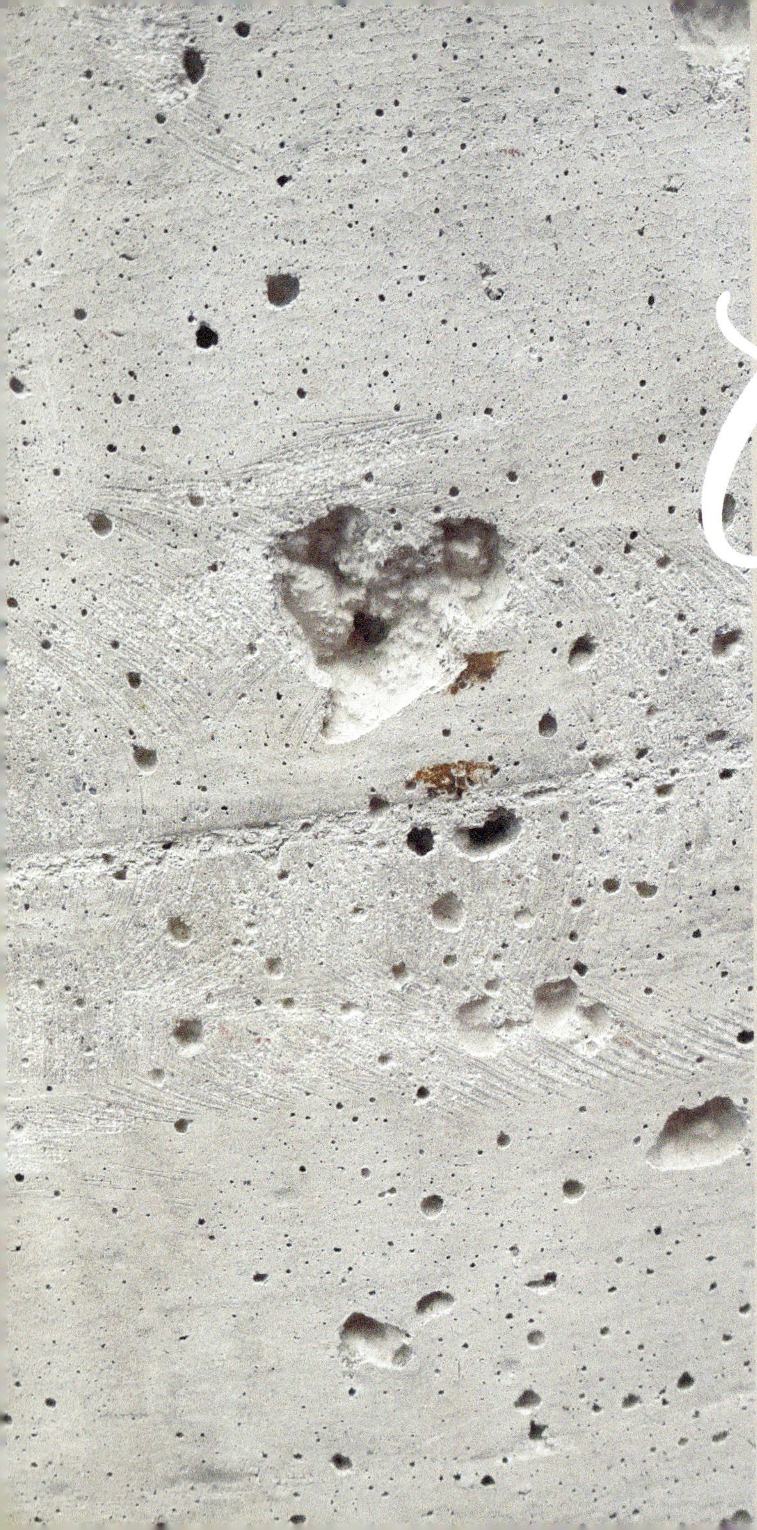

A concrete **heart** is so
perfectly permanent.
It won't change,
waiver or fade away.

Any time I look for it,
I'm guaranteed to see
it forever and a day.

Do you have a chip
on your shoulder
or are you just
chip,
chip,
chipping away
at my heart?

Is your **heart** healthy?

One day I was sitting in my favorite coffee shop
reflecting on my life's decisions
and having an introspective moment by myself.

My gaze goes down to my table and I grin as I see a wooden heart.

It never ceases to amaze me
how nature gives subtle reminders that we live to love and love to live.

What makes your **heart** smile?

This heart appears to be stuck in motion.
Is that possible? Think about it.

How can anything be “stuck” if it’s in “motion.”

Don’t let your **heart** try to fool you.

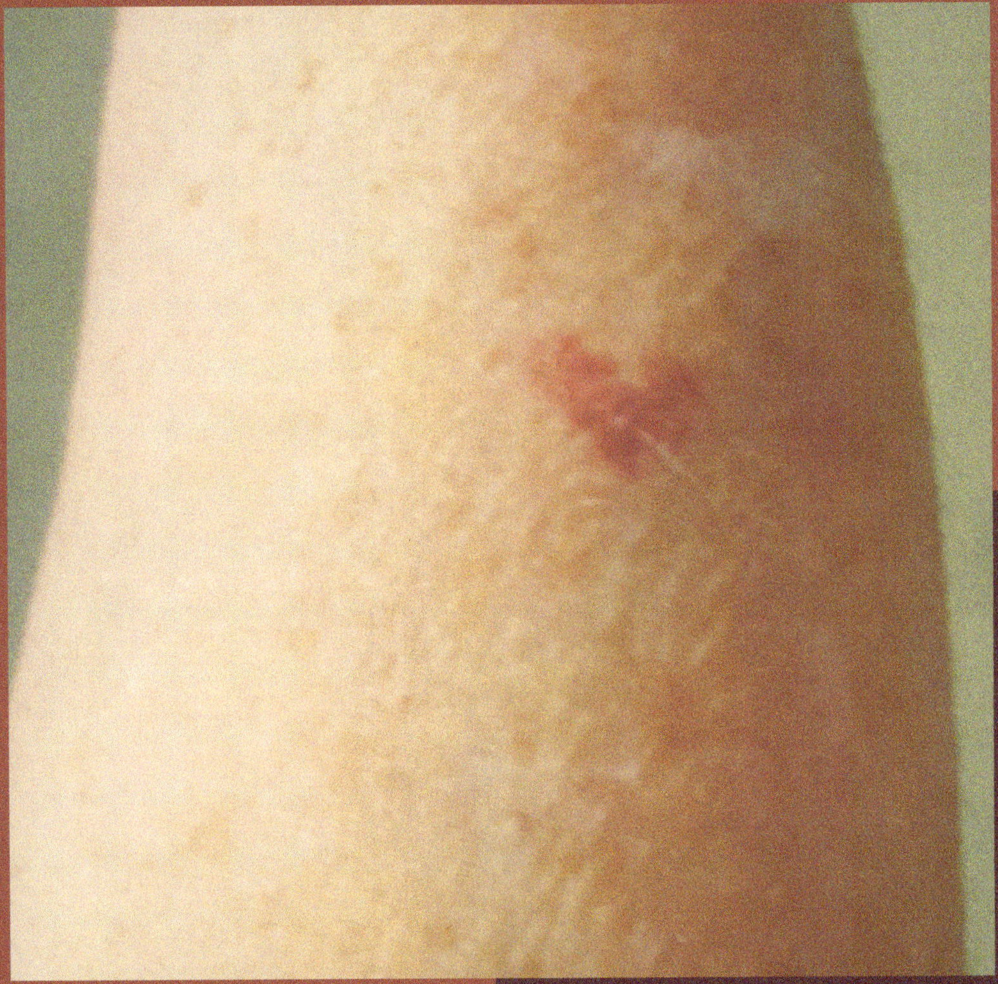

When your heart is bruised, how do you mend it?
Do you let the feeling fade
or stay away from what made it that way?

Heal your **heart.**

There's no reason to whine

when nature shows you a heart
that's being cast down from the sky.

I do believe this was one of the more unique places
to find a heart.

Beyond a shadow of doubt,
hearts signify that love is everywhere.

I

Is it a fur ball or is it lint?

Whatever the material,
it's proof that accidental hearts can be anywhere
and made of anything.

This is the definition of an unexpected **heart**.

H

Hearts can be sweet ... and they can be tart.

Satisfy what your **heart** craves.

Jenny Lynne is a lover of nature who fittingly lives in Denver, CO. While being very active in the community, she also spends a lot of time in nature. Because of her creative outlook and imaginativeness, the book *Hearts* was brought to life.

After several years of photographing accidental hearts created by nature, it became a passion and habit to notice them in unexpected places.

These pictures gave her an outlet to capture her wit, humor and sometimes seriousness by describing the emotions and perceptions that were evoked. At the same time, it brought about a sense of surrounding love and positive energy that was not hers to keep private but rather to share knowing that this topic is one with which everyone could identify.

Explore Jenny's website at: **www.JennyLynneBooks.com**

@JennyLynneBooks

@JennyLynneBooks

@JennyLynneBooks

@JennyLynneBooks

Tecate. B.C., Mexico (2017)

Denver, CO (2014)

Maui, HI (2016)

Morrison, CO (2014)

Denver, CO (2013)

Denver, CO (2011)

Golden, CO (2017)

Denver, CO (2013)

Colorado Springs, CO (2014)

Vail, CO (2015)

San Diego, CA (2010)

Aspen, CO (2014)

Denver, CO (2016)

Denver, CO (2016)

Denver, CO (2014)

Leadville, CO (2010)

Denver, CO (2013)

Tecate, B.C., Mexico (2017)

Tecate, B.C., Mexico (2017)

Tecate, B.C., Mexico (2017)

Denver, CO (2016)

Denver, CO (2013)

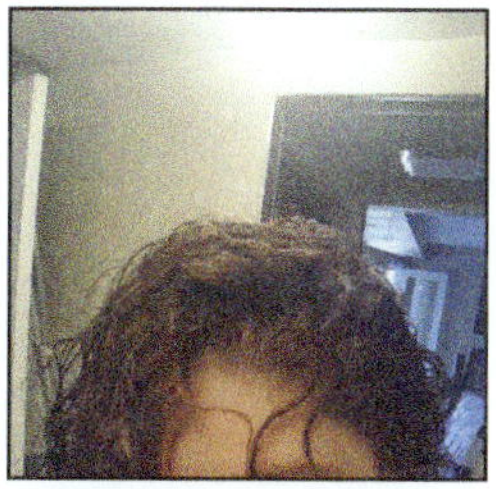
Denver, CO (2018)

Denver, CO (2013)

Mexico City, Mexico (2017)

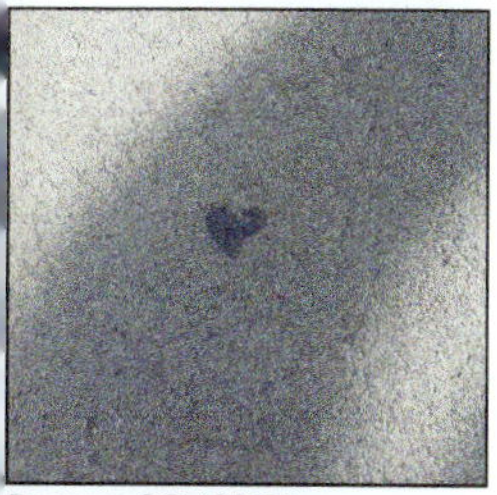
Denver, CO (2017)

Sante Fe, NM (2017)

Golden, CO (2016)

Denver, CO (2015)

Denver, CO (2012)

Sante Fe, NM (2017)

Tallahassee, FL (2014)

Vail, CO (2016)

Tecate. B.C., Mexico (2017)

Marble, CO (2016)

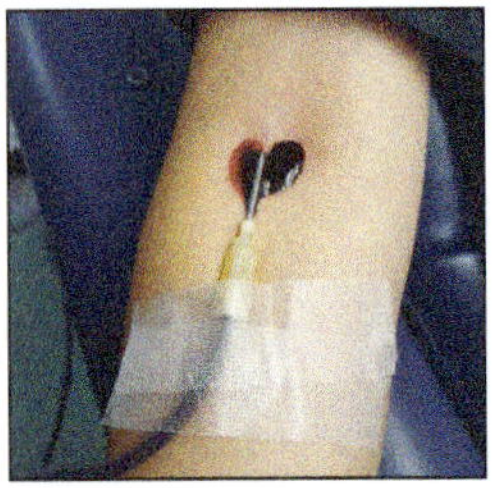
Denver, CO (2017)

Morrison, CO (2015)

Tecate, B.C., Mexico (2017)

San Ramon, CA (2011)

Golden, CO (2017)

Lakewood, CO (2017)

Denver, CO (2010)

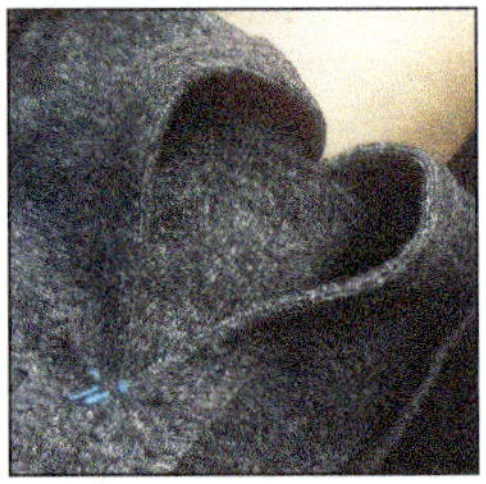
Denver, CO (2015)

Denver, CO (2018)

Aurora, CO (2012)

Denver, CO (2017)

Golden, CO (2017)

Golden, CO (2017)

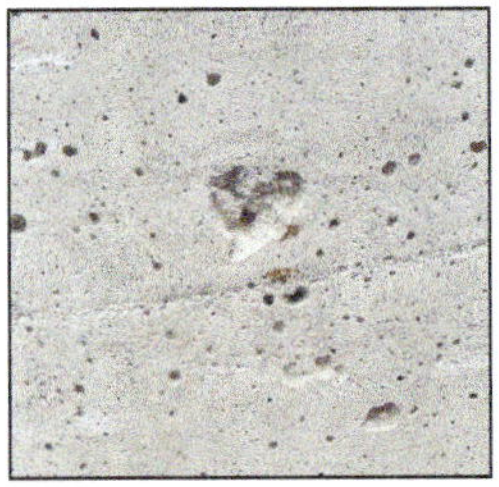
Cherry Creek, CO (2013)

Denver, CO (2012)

Dallas, TX (2016)

Denver, CO (2018)

Denver, CO (2014)

New York City, NY (2016)

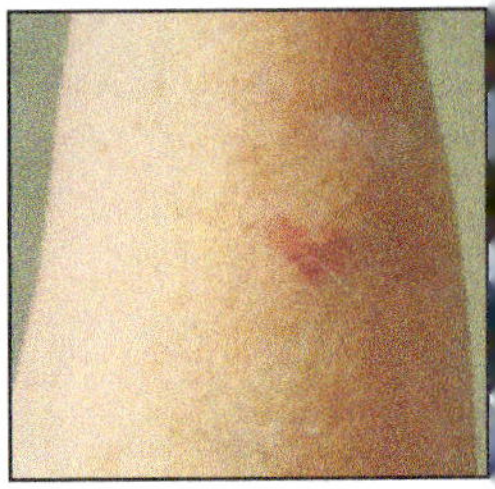
Denver, CO (2011)

Napa Valley, CA (2017)

Dallas, TX (2014)

Denver, CO (2018)

ANSWERS

Balance

First, use the balance to divide the 80 grams into two piles of 40 grams. Then divide one of the 40-gram piles in half. Now balance the 20 grams against the 7 grams produced by the two masses. The 13 grams that are removed from the balance form one pile. The 7 grams added to the 40 grams + 20 grams produces the larger pile of 67 grams.

Big Magic

The sum of the side is thirty-four, and the square looks like this:

1	11	6	16
8	14	3	9
15	5	12	2
10	4	13	7

Break It Up!

Nine toothpicks need to be removed as shown below.

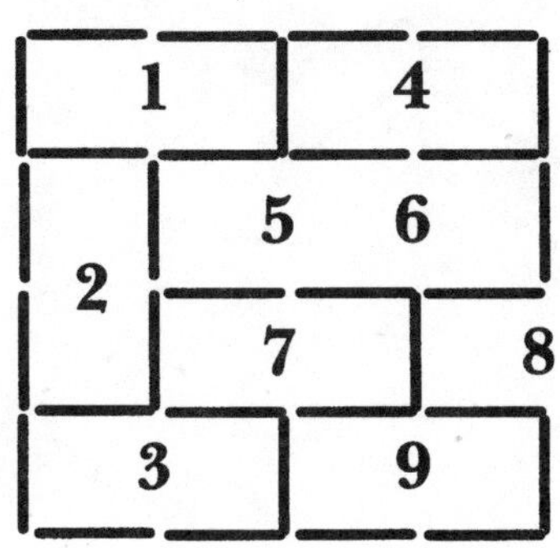

Breaking the Rules

Two inches. Each chalk piece will advance only half the distance covered by the ruler.

Breaking Up Is Hard to Do... Sometimes

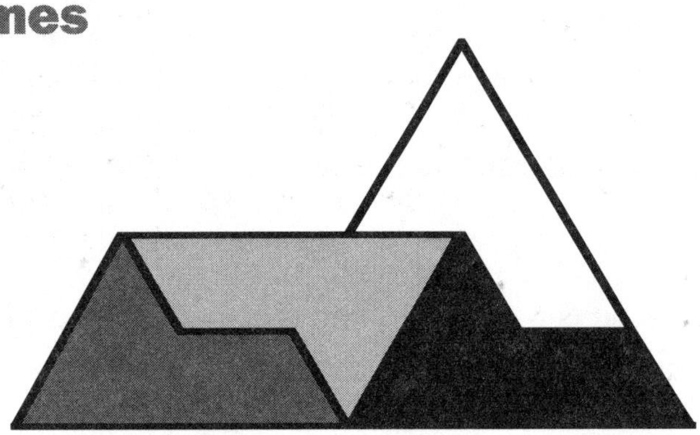

Bridge, Anyone?

The sticks below are arranged so that they support each other in a central triangle formed by overlapping and underlapping supports.

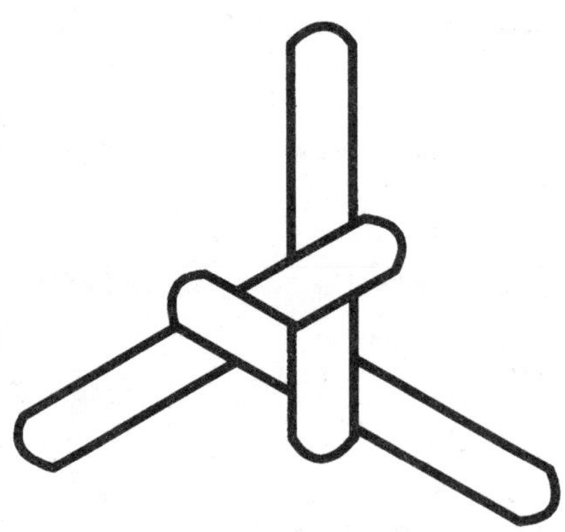

Cards, Anyone?

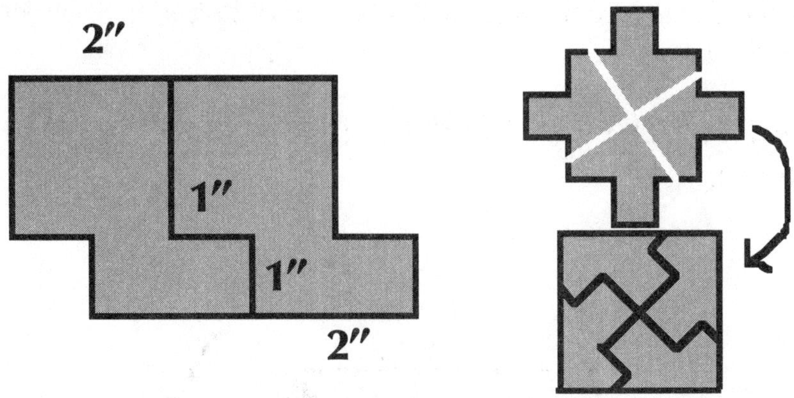

Change of Pace

a. either 5 pennies ($.05) + 4 nickels ($.20) + 1 quarter ($.25) = $.50; or 10 nickels ($.05) = $.50

b. 25 pennies ($.25) + 1 nickel ($.05) + 2 dimes ($.20) + 2 quarters ($.50) = $1.00

Check It Out

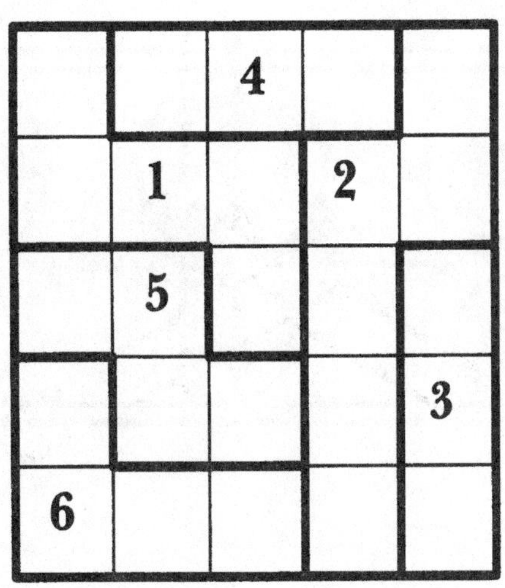

A Class Act

Seven students play only keyboards. A diagram helps illustrate and solve this problem.

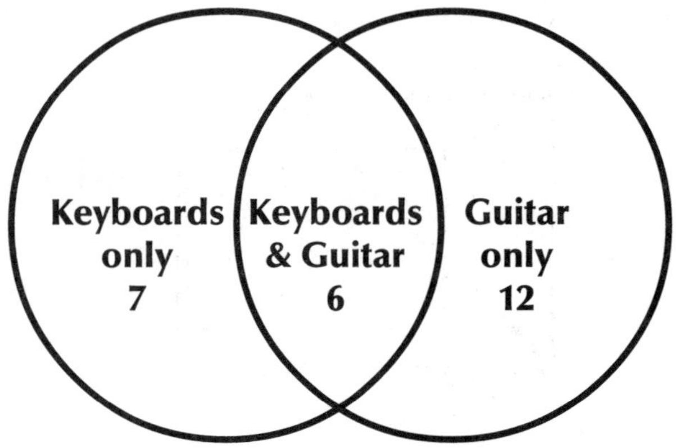

Coin Roll

The coins maintain their relative position to each other as they move along the track. What changes is the direction in which the coin images point.

Cool Cut

Make the cut from one corner straight across to the corners as shown below. Each side of this regular triangle that is formed is equal in length to the diagonal of the square.

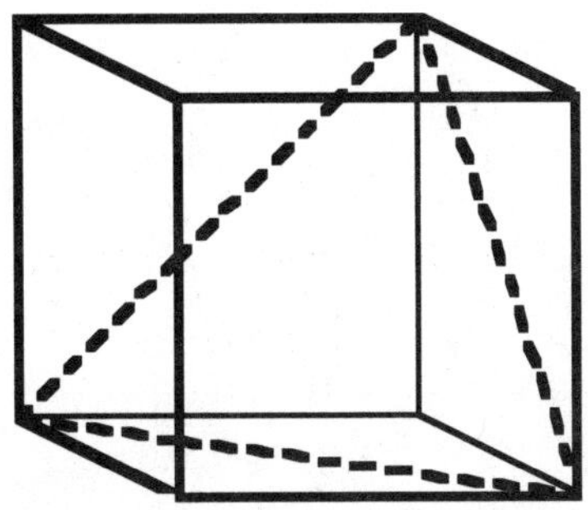

Doing Wheelies

Wheel A would be spinning at five revolutions per minute. Wheel B would be spinning at twenty revolutions per minute. The difference in speed results from the "gearing up" and the "gearing down" from the first wheel set to the second wheel set. The belts between the second and third wheel sets do not affect the spin.

Don't Stop Now

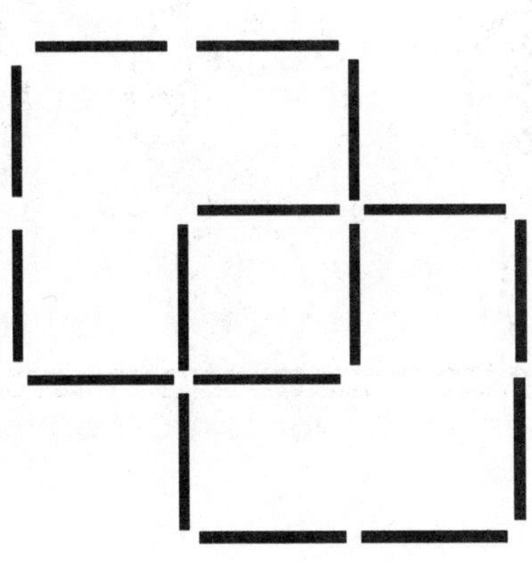

Exactly... Well, Almost

E. It is the mirror image of the other repeating (but rotating) design.

Face Lift

a. Eighteen faces.
b. Twenty-six faces.
c. Twenty-two faces.

A Game for Losers

By placing your "O" marker in either of the boxes indicated below, you are ensured a victory no matter where your opponent places his or her "X"s.

Get Set. Go!

150 miles long. In order to complete 30 miles of distance, the faster cyclist requires 1 hour of time while the slower cyclist needs 1.20 hours. Therefore, the time difference per 30 miles of travel is .20 hours. In order to increase the difference to 1 hour, multiple the 30 miles by 5.

Give Me Five

1111. Easy, unless of course you forget all it takes to solve this problem is to divide 5555 by 5!

Going Batty

The number of beetles captured on each successive night were 8, 14, 20, 26, and 32.

Good Guess

Forty-eight gumballs. Since two guesses were off by seven and no guesses were repeated, these values had to refer to numbers at the opposite extremes of the spread. The two extremes are 41 and 55. If you add 7 to one and take 7 away from the other, you arrive at the middle number of 48.

Here, Art, Art, Art

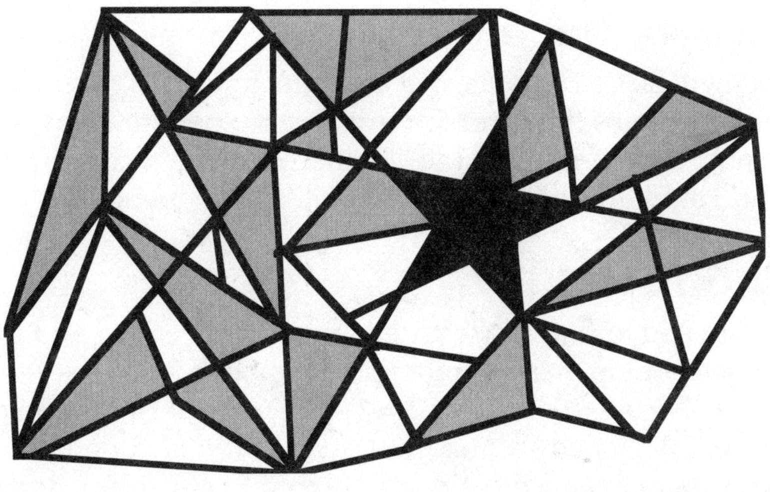

Here, Spot, Spot, Spot

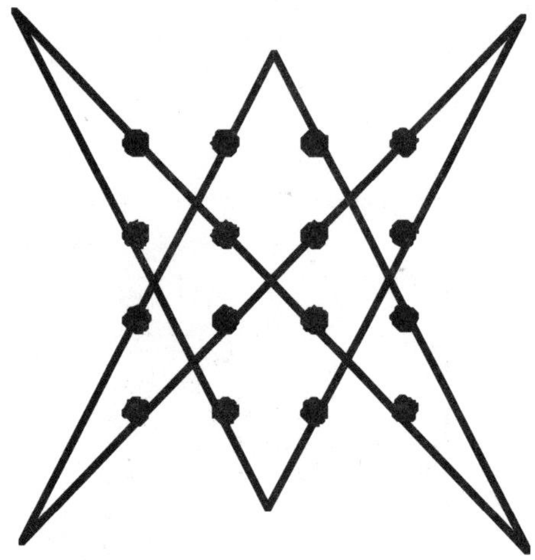

Iron Horse Race

The trains will be tied 3 hours after the faster train (or $4^1/_2$ hours after the slower train) begins the race. For example, if the trains travel 60 mph and 90 mph, the $4^1/_2$-hour journey for the slower train covers 270 miles, while the 3-hour journey for the faster train also covers 270 miles.

Keep On Tickin'

First you'll need to find out what each section needs to add to. To get this number, add up every number on the clock's face (1 + 2 + 3 + 4 + 5 + 6 + 7 + 8 + 9 + 10 + 11 + 12 = 78). Divide 78 by 3 and you'll get 26—the sum that each section must add to. The next part is relatively easy, since the numbers are already laid out in a ready-to-add pattern.

Keeping Time

Six hours. In 6 hours, the slow clock will be exactly 30 minutes behind while the fast clock will be exactly 30 minutes ahead of time.

Lasagna Cut

Each person gets one large and one small triangular piece.

Here's a slightly different pattern that produces four similarly shaped slices (if we assume the connecting points between the triangle pairs remain uncut).

Look Over Here

b

The direction of the look is based upon the number of neighboring eyes that are in contact with the eye's circumference. Eyes that "touch" three other circles (such as the circle in question) have a pupil that points to the right.

Magic Star

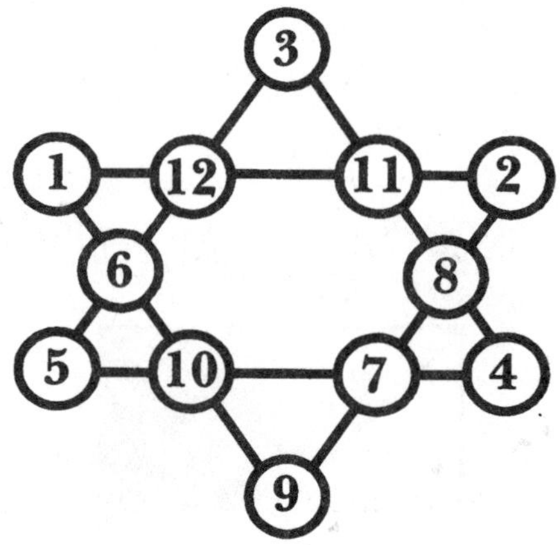

Main Attraction

Take either bar (it doesn't matter which one) and touch one end of the bar to the middle of the other bar. If the bar you are holding is a magnet, then its pole will cause the nonmagnetized bar to move. If, however, you've picked up the nonmagnetized bar, no attraction will occur. That's because neither of the poles is being touched.

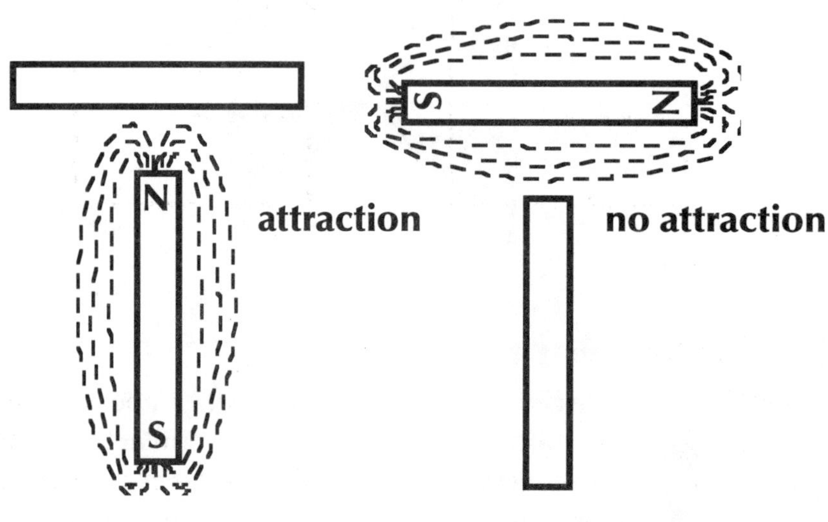

Melt Down

The level of water will not change. Although the top of the cube floats above the surface of the water, the amount of water in the entire ice cube can fill a space equal to the dimensions occupied by the part of the cube that is under the water's surface. In other words, as the ice cube turns to water, it produces the same amount of water as the space occupied by the submerged part of the cube.

Mind Bend

Place three parallel cuts in the card. Two of the cuts should be positioned on one side, while a single central cut should be made on the opposite side (as shown below). Then place a twist in the card so that half of the upper surface is formed by the "bottom-side" of the card. For extra fun, you might want to tape the folded card by all of its edges to the desk (making it more difficult to uncover the baffling "twist").

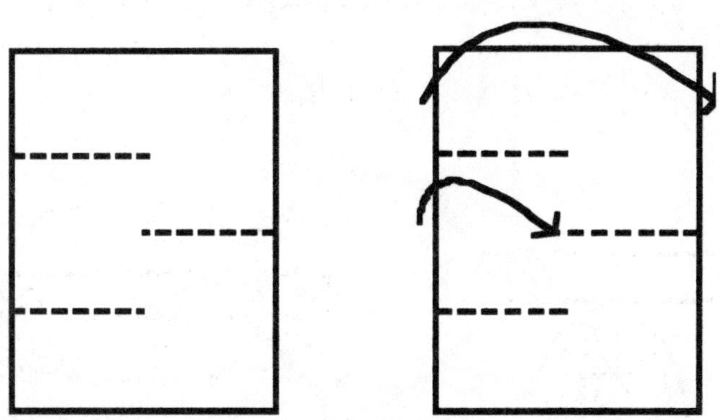

More Cheese

No. Six cuts are the fewest number of cuts needed to produce the twenty-seven smaller cubes. Stacking doesn't result in fewer cuts. Think of it this way: that innermost cube of the twenty-seven must be formed by a cut on each of its six sides.

Mind Slice

The angle of the cut will not affect the shape at all. All cuts will produce faces that are perfect circles. The feature that does change with the cutting angle is the circle size.

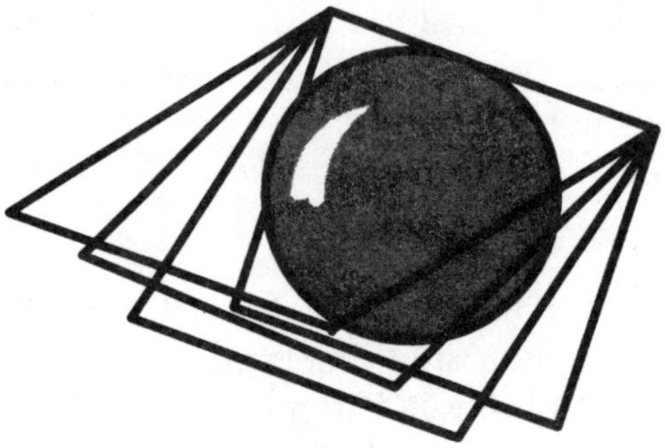

More Coinage

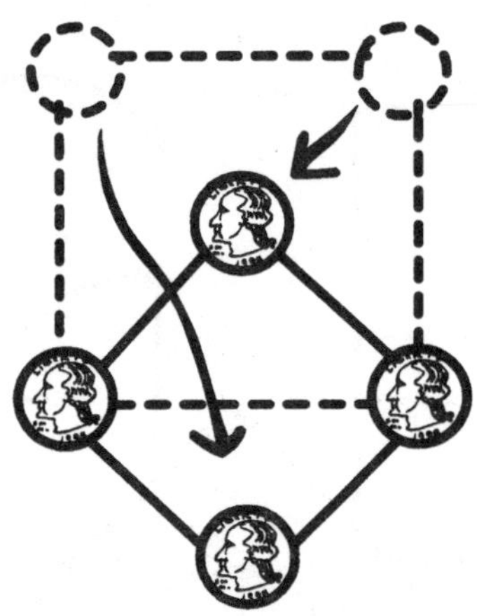

More Wheelies

480 revolutions. Since wheel B's rim is four times longer than wheel A's rim, it spins at one-fourth the speed (4 rps). Likewise, wheel B's rim is twice as long as wheel C's rim. Therefore, wheel C's rim spins twice as fast (8 rps). In 1 minute, C wheel will complete 60 x 8 revolutions, or 480 revolutions.

Number Blocks

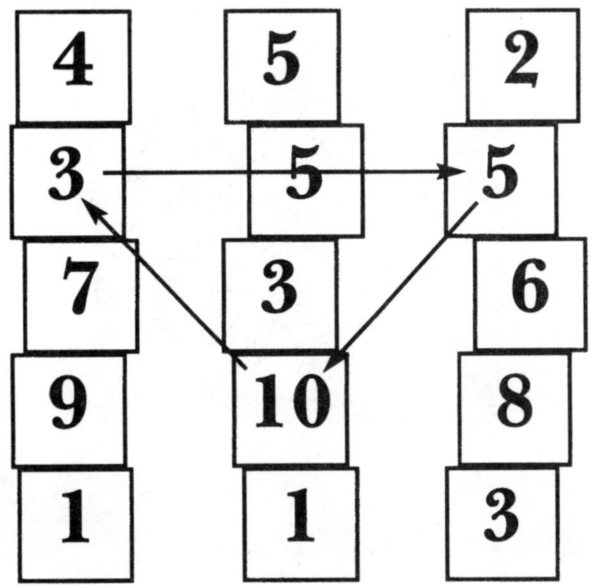

One Way Only

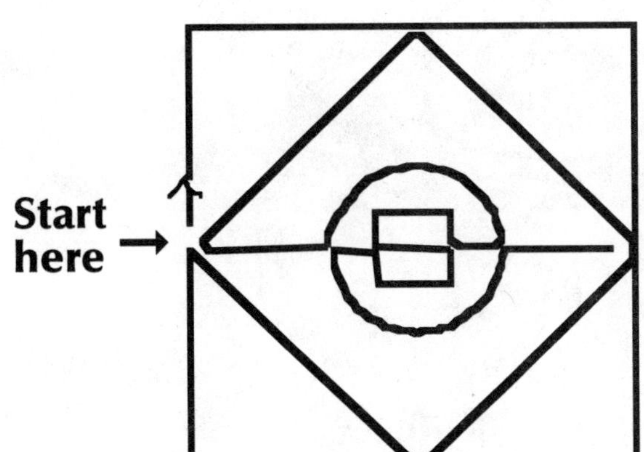

Parts of a Whole

Puzzle Paths

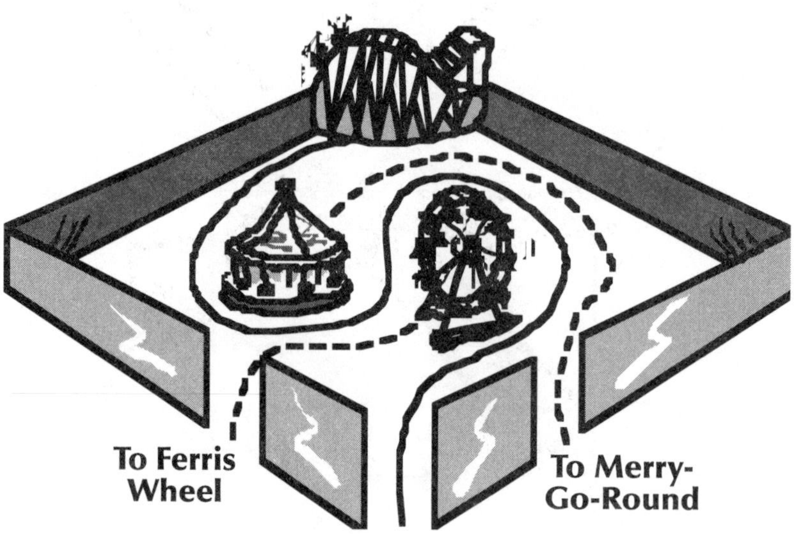

Oops, I Wasn't Concentrating

It is weaker than the original solution. In order to have the original concentration, Anthony would have to add grape juice that is $2\frac{1}{2}$ times the regular strength.

Raises and Cuts

They are now both earning the exact same amount. To prove this, let's take a sample first-week salary of $100 for both Moe and Bo. After the first adjustment, Moe earned $110 while Bo earned $90. During the second adjustment, Moe was cut by $11 to $99. At the same time, Bo was increased by $9 to $99.

Runaway Runway

Six intersections as shown below.

Roller Coaster, Roll!

Young Ed. The car that travels along the curved slope accelerates faster. This extra speed results from the quick drop in the path that allows the car to quickly pick up speed as the car moving down the straight slope accelerates at a slower and more uniform rate.

Satellite Surveyor

80 square miles. If you examine the dissected grid, you'll uncover that the composite shapes include side-by-side pairs that can be joined to form four squares. The total area is 20 x 20, or 400 square miles. Each of the five identical squares contains one-fifth, or 80 square miles.

Say Cheese

Make three cuts that divide the cube into eight smaller but equal cubes. Each of these eight cubes has a side length of 1 inch to produce a surface area of 6 square inches. The sum of the eight cube surface areas is 48 square inches.

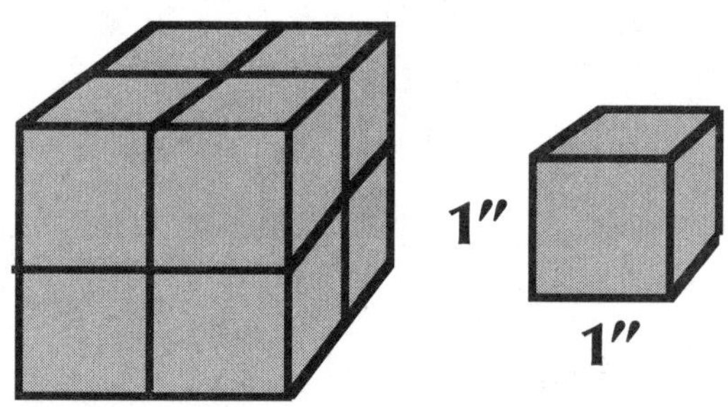

Screws in the Head

As the threads turn, they will produce a counterclockwise motion in the gear of the tuning post. This motion will decrease the tension in the string to produce a note of lower pitch.

Screwy Stuff

The threads of screw A form a spiral that would "go into" the wood block. In contrast, the opposite spiral of screw B would result in this screw moving out of the wooden block.

Separation Anxiety

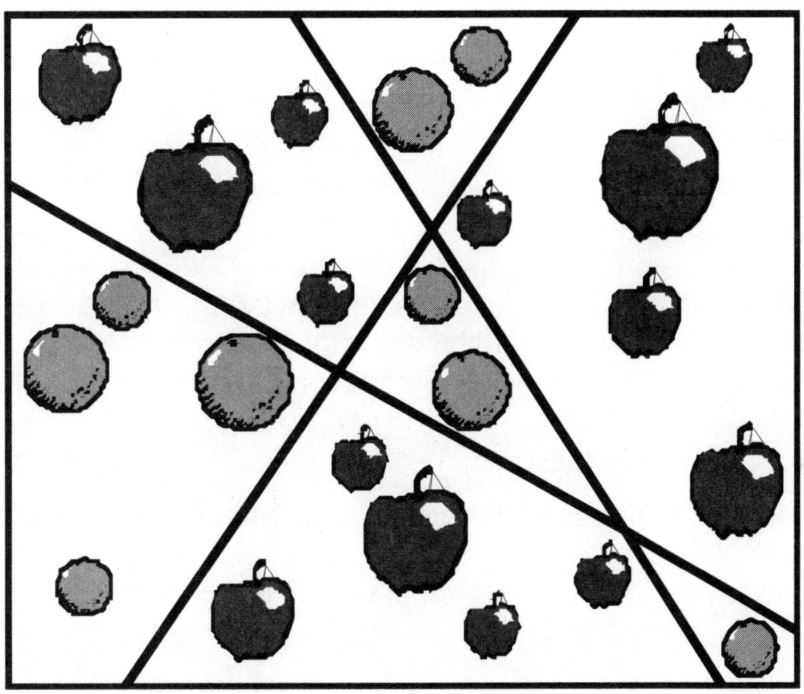

Sequence Grid

Triangle. The grid is filled by a series of number sequences. The first sequence consists of only one member—a square. The second and adjoining sequence includes a square + circle. The third sequence expands to include a square + circle + triangle. The complete sequence from which the "?" can be determined is square + circle + triangle + triangle + circle + circle.

Some Things Never Change

7 + 49 + 343 + 2401 + 16,807 = 19,607.

Spiral^2

The complete path from entrance to center is 5000 feet. To obtain this distance, determine the total area of the structure (10,000 square feet). Now mentally unroll the spiral. Divide the 10,000-square-foot area by the area associated with one foot of forward travel. Since the corridor is 2 feet wide, the area for a single foot of forward motion is 2 square feet. Dividing 10,000 by 2, we arrive at the total distance of 5000 feet.

The Race Is On

The wheel with the centrally placed lead will accelerate fastest. This behavior reflects a property of physics that ice skaters execute during their moves. As a skater spins, the speed of the spin can be adjusted by altering his or her distribution of weight. As the arms extend, the spinning skater slows. As the arms draw in, the spin accelerates.

Sum Puzzle

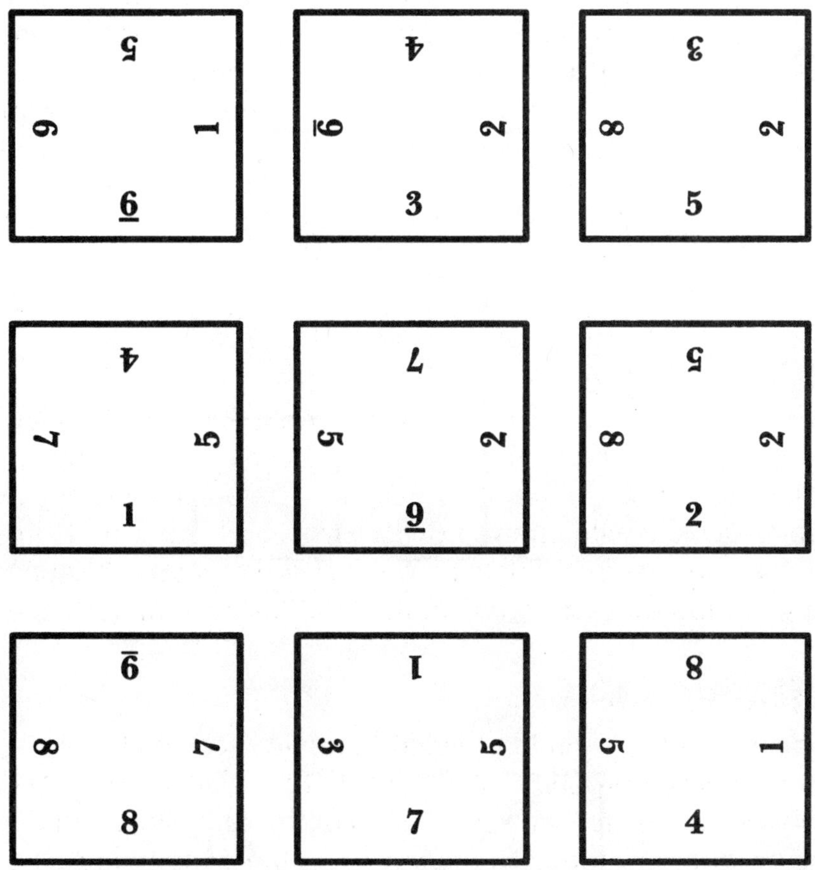

Surrounded by Squares

Thirteen squares.

Take 'em Away

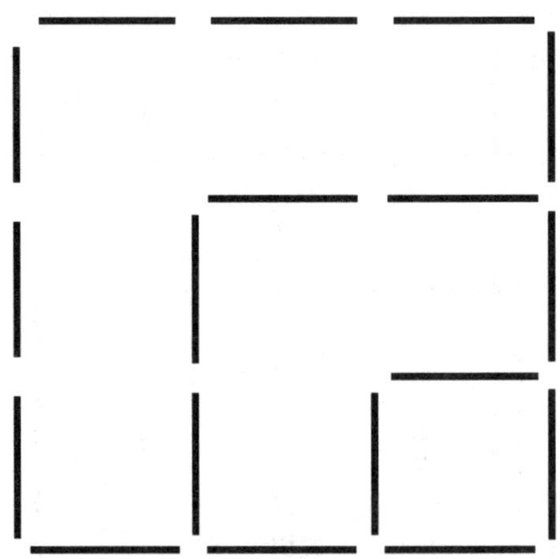

Take Your Pick

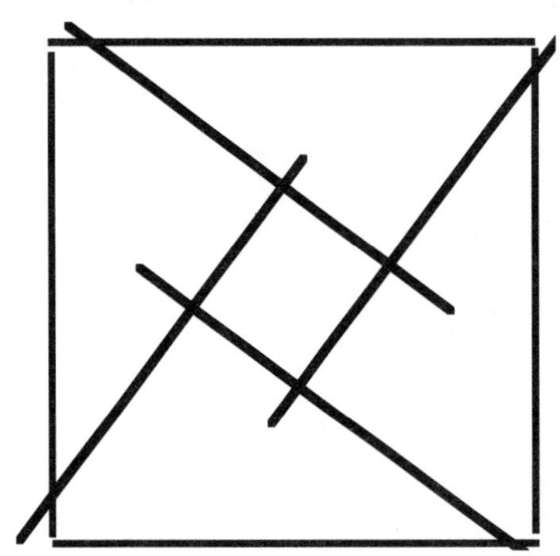

Thick As a Brick

Sixty bricks. You don't have to count all of the bricks. Just count the bricks in the uppermost layer (twelve) and multiply by the number of layers (five) so that you arrive at a total number of sixty bricks.

Time on Your Hands

7:22. For each given time, the minute hand advances a quarter of a complete counterclockwise rotation, while the hour hand advances three-eighths of a complete counterclockwise rotation. The final arrangement looks like this:

Togetherness

The computer weighs 16 pounds and its monitor weighs 32 pounds.

Trying Times

Eight unique triangles as shown below.

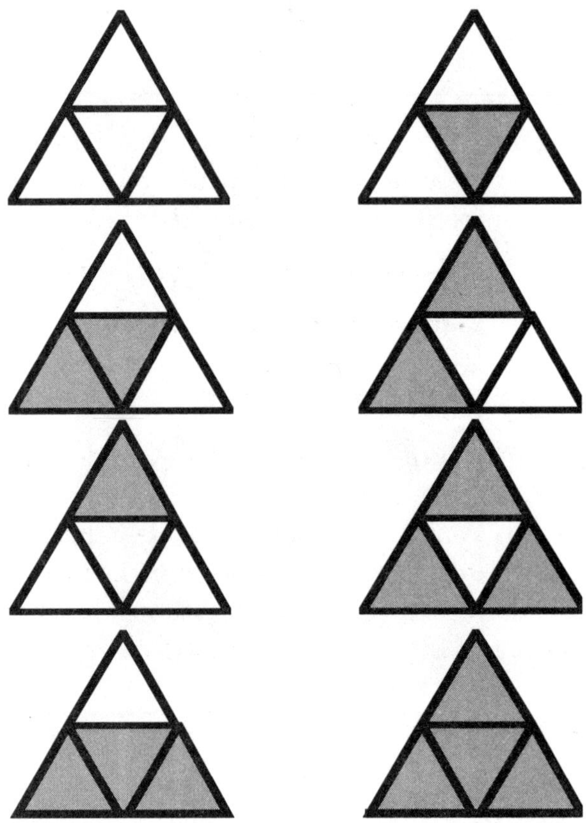

Turn, Turn, Turn

F.

Weighty Problem

120 pounds. If she needs to add "half of her weight" to get her full weight, then the weight that she does tell (60 pounds) must be half of her total. Therefore, 60 pounds is half of her weight. 60 + 60 = 120 pounds. If this doesn't seem right, just work it backwards starting with the 120 pounds.

What's the Angle?

a. Three copies of this shape are positioned as shown here.

Whale of a Problem

Two minutes. The amount of time needed to catch the seals doesn't change. Since two whales can catch two seals in 2 minutes, it is logical to assume that a single whale can catch one seal in that same period of time. Likewise, three whales can catch three seals in 2 minutes. As long as the number of whales is equal to the number of seals, the time doesn't change. Therefore, ten killer whales will also take 2 minutes to catch ten seals.

Wrap It Up

d. Here's what you see as you unwrap the folds.

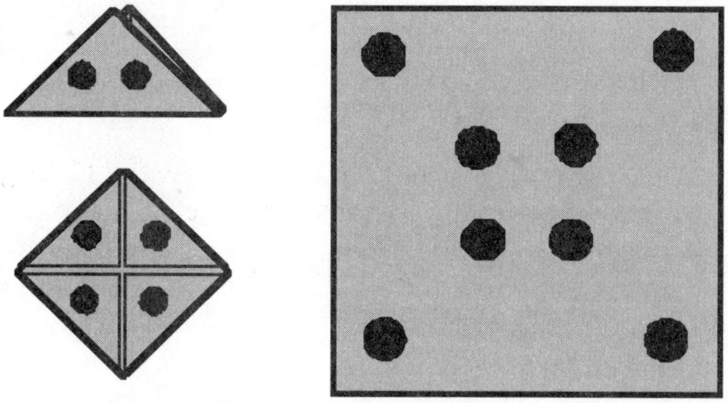

INDEX

Answers appear on pages in *italics*.